CHRISTABEL BIELENBERG AND
NAZI GERMANY

—— HEINEMANN ——

HISTORY
EYEWITNESS

EDITED WITH AN INTRODUCTION
AND ADDITIONAL MATERIAL BY
JANE SHUTER

Heinemann

Published by Heinemann Library,
an imprint of Heinemann Publishers (Oxford) Ltd,
Halley Court, Jordan Hill, Oxford OX2 8EJ

OXFORD LONDON EDINBURGH MADRID
ATHENS BOLOGNA PARIS MELBOURNE
SYDNEY AUCKLAND SINGAPORE TOKYO
IBADAN NAIROBI HARARE GABORONE
PORTSMOUTH NH (USA)

Selection and additional material
© Heinemann Educational 1994

98 97 96 95 94 93
10 9 8 7 6 5 4 3 2 1

British Library Cataloguing in Publication Data
Christabel Bielenberg and Nazi Germany. –
(History Eyewitness Series)
I. Shuter, Jane II. Series
943.086092

ISBN 0 431 07151 9

Designed by Green Door Design Ltd, map by Jeff Edwards
Printed in China

Acknowledgements
The publishers would like to thank the following for
permission to reproduce photographs:

Andromeda Oxford Ltd.: p.9
Derek Banes/Imperial War Museum/©Time-Life International: p.7
Bildarchiv Preussicher Kulturbesitz: p.14
Bundesarchiv, Koblenz: p.42
Gunn Brinson: p.21
Hulton Deutsch Collection Ltd.: pp.13, 16
Imperial War Museum: pp.23, 30
Landesbildsteine, Berlin: p.33
Popperfoto: cover and pp.26, 29
Süddeutscher Verlag: p.15
Topham Picture Source: pp.39, 41
Ullstein Bilderdienst: pp.11, 37, 45
Weidenfeld and Nicolson Archives: p.25
Weiner Library: p.35

The cover photograph shows a Nazi rally and a portrait of
Christabel Bielenberg.

Every effort has been made to contact copyright holders of material
reproduced in this book. Any omissions will be rectified in
subsequent printings if notice is given to the publisher.

Note to the reader

In this book some of the words are printed in **bold** type. This indicates that the
word is listed in the glossary on pages 46–7. The glossary gives a brief explanation
of words that may be new to you.

CONTENTS

Introduction

Christabel Bielenberg

Christabel Bielenberg was born in 1909. She had English and Irish lords as relations and was the niece of Lord Northcliffe. She was brought up in 'comparative luxury', and her education included some time at a 'finishing school' in Paris. She studied singing in Germany and married Peter Bielenberg, a German lawyer, in 1934. This is the point at which this book begins. They had three sons, Nicky, John and Christopher. After the war, Christabel went back to England, while Peter stayed behind in Germany to try to sort things out, and to find Clarita, Adam von Trott's wife. Christabel became a British citizen again, returned to Germany as a war correspondent for the *Observer*, and finally managed to get papers to allow Peter to move to England. The children went to boarding schools and Peter and Christabel tried to find somewhere to live. Peter was in a road accident and, during his difficult convalescence, Christabel became ill. When both were recovered enough they went to look for somewhere to live in Ireland. In 1949 they moved into a dilapidated farm in Tullow, Ireland, armed with a copy of *Teach Yourself Farming*. They still live there.

Nazi Germany

How did the Nazis come to power in Germany? They used the German political system, which, because of the way elections were held, meant that no one party ran the country. The Nazis could take power with just a few elected members, if those members could get powerful jobs in the Government. Looking back on the Nazi rise to power now, knowing what was to come later, it is possible to see that Adolf Hitler and the Nazis would want to take over Europe, and kill Jews. But, at the time, at the beginning of their rise to power, they sounded more moderate. They promised 'Bread and Work', both of which were in short supply in Germany in the early 1930s. Even when they started to take land, it was land which many Germans felt was part of Germany anyway, land they had lost at the Treaty of Versailles. The Treaty of Versailles, signed in 1919, marked the end of the First World War (1914–18), which Germany lost. The American President, Woodrow Wilson, had put forward a fourteen point plan for peace, which was fair to all sides; but the French and British were not in a mood to be fair. The war had caused a horrendous loss of life on all sides; their view was that it was Germany's fault, so Germany should pay. The Treaty of Versailles was very hard on Germany. Germany had a lot of land taken away, and had to pay a lot of money as a sort of fine, which caused the **inflation** of the 1920s. In 1924–8 Germany seemed to be recovering from all this. The Nazis had little political support. Then, in 1929, the world economy collapsed. Inflation and unemployment followed. Germans became discontented. The Nazis played on this. A few members were elected and one of them, Hitler, managed to get the job of Chancellor. The Nazis took over.

N

NORWAY

Riga

Cuxhaven
● Hamburg

● Graudenz

◆ Ravensbrück

POLAND

HOLLAND

Oranienburg ◆
● Berlin

◆ Chelmno

● Magdeburg

G E R M A N Y

● Körle

Aachen

River Rhine

BELGIUM

Treblinka ◆

Sobibor ◆

Belzec ◆

SUDETENLAND

CZECHOSLOVAKIA

Auschwitz ◆

● Nuremburg

Black
Forest ● Stuttgart

FRANCE

Schoenwald
Rohrbach ● ● Tuttlingen
Funwangen ● Munich
● Donaueschingen
Bodensee

AUSTRIA

SWITZERLAND

*This map shows the places that
Christabel Bielenberg mentions in her
story.*

Key

Land Germany kept under
the Treaty of Versailles

Borders of Greater
Germany in 1939

Rail line connections

● Towns and cities

◆ Concentration camps

0   100 miles

0   100 km

CHAPTER 1

Not a Good Swap?

NATIONAL SOCIALISM

The National Socialist Party grew out of the German Workers' Party, set up in Munich in 1919. Hitler joined the party in 1919 and was soon in a position of power. It was he who gave the Party its new name: the National Socialist German Workers' Party. This was shortened to 'Nazi'. Its symbol was a black swastika in a white circle on a red background. It was Hitler who set up the storm-troopers, called 'brownshirts'. He was a great believer in the power of uniforms, songs and rallies. The storm-troopers broke up the meetings of rival parties, often getting into violent fights. In November 1923 Hitler and the Nazis tried to seize power. They failed. Hitler was sent to prison. Here he wrote *Mein Kampf*. When he got out he was ready to take over the Nazi Party again. This time he had a new tactic, getting political power by election not by force. The National Socialists appealed to people who were hit hardest by the depression from 1929 to 1933.

At four o'clock in the afternoon, on 29 September, 1934, I became a German citizen. In a basement office of the German **Embassy** in London I exchanged my British passport for its German equivalent – a nondescript brown booklet with a disdainful looking eagle stamped in black on its drab cardboard cover. The eagle clutched a **swastika** emblem in its skinny claws. As the German Ambassador gave me my German passport and locked away my British one he made a rather unexpected remark. 'You've not made a very good swap, I'm afraid,' he said. Neither Peter's parents nor mine thought the marriage was a good thing, though both sets of parents put a brave face on it at the wedding. And Peter and I gave little thought, as we drove off on our honeymoon, to the warnings from both sides that had been issued all through our two-year-long courtship.

I met Peter in Hamburg in 1932, when I was staying with a nice family who had one son, Hans, who believed that the answer to all Germany's ills was National Socialism, and that the cause of them was the Jews. Over cups of cocoa, with picture postcards of Hitler in many different poses pinned to his walls, Hans told me why National Socialism was the only thing which could save Germany from complete chaos. Did I know that the 1914–18 war had not been lost by the German soldiers at the front, but by **decadent** politicians at home? His father had fought bravely for years, but had had to see the badges of rank torn from the shoulders of his brother officers when they returned to the **Fatherland**. Had I ever heard of President Wilson's Fourteen Points? Those terms of surrender which had persuaded the young warriors to lay down their arms, only to be confronted a year later with the shameful Treaty of Versailles? Such a peace should never have been accepted. His father now only had a humble job, they could not afford a cook. Unless the Nazis came to power there would be no hope of a job for him when he left university, for they had no influential Jewish friends. Only 3% of the population of Hamburg was Jewish, he said, but the Jews ran everything – 40% of all doctors were Jews, 30% of all lawyers, even 10% of all judges. The shops, the banks, the businesses – too many of them were run by Jews and Jews always stuck together. His parents had lost everything they had in the **inflation**, but not so the Jews; they had flourished since the war.

Hans was a gentle fellow by nature, but sometimes, when he really got going, he rose to his feet, face flushed, and struck poses very like those in the postcards on the walls. He lent me Hitler's *Mein Kampf* to read, and I kampfed four pages before I gave up. He then took me to some Party meetings, which I found far more entertaining. Before leaving we passed the rows of tables set up in the side aisles to see how many people were queueing up to sign for Party membership.

On one occasion, in the autumn of 1932, I even managed to get Peter to come with me. Hitler himself was to speak at an open air rally. It was held – appropriately, as Peter pointed out – in Hamburg's zoo. A huge area had been **cordoned off**. Rows of burly **storm-troopers** wedged the milling crowds into orderly rectangles. Peter survived the community singing, the rolling of the drums, the National and Party anthems. Then Hitler began to speak. My ears were hardly used to his Austrian accent when I was marched out of the enclosure by a disgusted Peter. Up against the giraffe-house, well within earshot of Party members in their familiar brown pill-box hats, who were rattling collection boxes under the noses of late-comers, he made one of his rare political pronouncements; it caused a stop to the rattling as they heard it. 'You may think the Germans are political idiots, Chris,' he said very loudly and very firmly, 'and you may be right, but I can assure you that they won't be so stupid as to fall for that clown.'

Even in the early 1930s The Nazi Party was thinking of long-term rule. They started to try to catch children early. Young children were being taught the Hitler salute and Nazi propaganda from 1933. Older children became absorbed into the various branches of the Hitler Youth movement. By the end of 1933, 47% of boys aged between ten and fourteen had joined the Hitler Youth, and 38% of those between fourteen and eighteen. Girls were less attracted to the movement. Only 15% of those between ten and fourteen joined the female equivalent of the Hitler Youth and only 8% of the older age group.

There were also less obvious attempts to influence children's lives, like the toys below. The figure on the left is Hitler. His arm could be moved up and down to perform the Nazi salute. The flags all have swastikas on them. The children carrying the smaller flags are members of the Hitler Youth movement.

CHAPTER 2

Hitler's Rise to Power

Three months later, on 30 January, 1933, Hitler became Germany's Chancellor. I was in England and read about it in the newspapers. I remember feeling rather pleased for Hans. I noticed that there were only two other National Socialists in the Cabinet; Hitler was hemmed in by respectable figures. I was glad that Hans would get his chance, but was also sure that in a month or so he, and everyone else, would be disillusioned. There would, as was usual in Germany, be yet another change of Government. But events in Germany now moved very fast. The burning of the **Reichstag**, the banning of the Communist Party, the last free elections, the Enabling Laws, the dissolution of Trade Unions and all other political parties – the whole process was over and done with by July of that year. It took Hitler just six months to manoeuvre himself and his party to power.

During those six months Peter and I became engaged. Peter was in his last year of law school. Some of his Jewish friends broke off their studies to leave while the going was good. But most stayed on, unable to believe, as yet, that Germany was about to turn against them. It was true that groups of rowdy storm-troopers roamed the flag-plastered streets of Hamburg, celebrating their political victory. It was also true that being seen with a Jew now caused taunting, even a street brawl, but Peter was fit enough to cope with these, and I wonder if he did not sometimes encourage them, to let off steam. But it was not until later that I felt what Peter already felt – something very nasty indeed might have come to stay.

We moved to London for the next part of Peter's legal training. It was a well-timed move; our first child would be born there and we could claim British citizenship for him. In our time away things got worse. When we returned we found many of the young people dressed in Hitler Youth uniform, the boys with clipped hair, the girls with massive plaits. The hideous Nazi flag flapped from every public building. The atmosphere had changed. Fear of unemployment, civil war and inflation had been replaced by an air of prosperity; while most people I met did not accept everything about the Nazis, they all said there was quite a lot to be said for how they ran the country. What had Hitler provided to persuade the Germans to give up their freedom so happily? Well, there was something for everyone in his political stew pot. Work for the unemployed, an army for the generals, a phoney religion for the gullible, a strident manner in foreign affairs for those who still **smarted** under the indignity of the lost war. Hitler knew he needed the support of the middle class, so he threw up a smoke-screen of respectability around everything that he did. But there were also **detention camps** and carefully broadcast hints about what was in store for anyone who enquired too closely about Hitler's methods, let alone openly disapproved of them.

ARBEIT BROT DRUM LISTE 1

A National Socialist Party election poster. It promises 'arbeit' (work) and 'brot' (bread). This poster, unlike some others, shows a 'brown shirt' in his brown cap with the swastika, as an intimidating figure. The implication here is that the work and bread will be got by whatever means are needed, even force.

STEPS TO WAR

From 1933–6 Hitler tried to seem a peacemaker abroad. He wanted to make sure he controlled Germany and had its war industry set up and producing, before acting.

Then, in 1935, with his war machine working well, Hitler re-occupied the Rhineland (which had been taken from Germany by the Treaty of Versailles at the end of the First World War). Britain and France did nothing. So when Hitler was invited, by a Nazi who had become Chancellor of Austria (once ruled by Germany) to take over Austria, he did so. Britain and France still did nothing. So Hitler invaded part of Czechoslovakia (once ruled by Germany) called the Sudetenland. This time France and Britain objected. They had a meeting with Hitler in Munich. They said they would let him keep the Sudetenland, as long as he went no further. He signed the agreement. He broke it. By the time he had taken Czechoslovakia and was marching on Poland, France and Britain knew they had to go to war to stop him going further.

Between 1935 and 1938 Peter and I came to see that we could not stay in Germany. At first it was possible to avoid joining the Party, attending rallies and so on. But as the régime got into gear and spread its tentacles throughout the whole fabric of public life it got more and more difficult. We learned to believe only what we saw with our own eyes and trusted only a few close friends. We decided to emigrate to Ireland. Then came the Munich Agreement and Hitler was forced to change his tactics. His storm-troopers erupted into violence. Anarchy was back on the streets and there could be no pretending that Hitler had not know about it. He was revelling in the whole thing, piling insult on insult, law and law against the Jews still living in Germany; saying this was the will of the German people.

CHAPTER 3

Moving to Berlin

A friend of ours, Adam von Trott, returned from Berlin to say we would be wrong to leave Germany now – the tide was turning, Hitler would be **ousted** and reliable people would be needed to work in a **civilian** government after Hitler's arrest. The thought of being able to do something positive sent our spirits soaring. I had Hitler behind bars and a new era dawning even before I had planned our move to Berlin. Peter applied for a job in the Ministry of Economics in Berlin. He had to apply for Party membership to get it, but we hoped that by the time it came through it would be comfortably out of date. As I moved between England, Hamburg and Berlin in the spring and summer of 1939 it was like moving between different planets. Berlin was an exciting city, a capital city and while I could take or leave the place itself, from the pine trees of the Grunewald to the bug-ridden area around the Alexander Platz, the people were irrepressible and charming. I wanted to live in the city, but had decided that, for the sake of the children, we needed a house with a garden. This meant I had to settle for one of the suburbs – Berlin-Dahlem.

The old and the new Ministries, the Embassies, the Reichs Chancellery, the headquarters of the Armed Forces, of the police and the Gestapo, all the power and **paraphernalia** surrounding the dictatorship was concentrated in Berlin. Like a magnet it attracted anyone who wanted to play the game of politics. Here you could see clearly that in Germany something had gone terribly wrong with the works. It had become like a prison turned inside out; the criminals in command, noisy and ruthless. Confronting them were the old established administrators of law and order who had stayed in their posts in 1933, and were still part of all branches of the administration. Driven by their principles as professionals and a repugnance for what was happening to their country, they had tried to keep hold of as much power and influence as they could.

No one, not even his closest associates, had ever really penetrated Hitler's curious mind. He was a lone operator but, as soon as his instructions took on the tangible form of memos and instructions, there was a well-established grapevine. When we arrived in Berlin in February, 1939, the grapevine was certain that Hitler was preparing for war in the autumn. He'd hardly finished signing the Munich Agreement before beginning his plans to invade Czechoslovakia; Poland was bound to be next – there were no bounds to his ultimate ambitions. He thought that if he marched east neither France nor Britain would oppose him. The only opposition that might defeat him was among the civilians in Germany – an opposition that Peter and Adam flung themselves into at once. There was no time to lose. And I? I finally decided that, politics or not, there would still be room for someone to cook the odd meal and look for a house with a garden.

Berlin was frantic, England was peaceful. Many people were still not sure what to make of Hitler. Not so my father. I talked earnestly about the opposition to Hitler in Germany; he listened sympathetically – but went on building his air-raid shelter. We moved into our house; Poland was invaded; war was declared. On the night war broke out I could not sleep. I remember every second, every tick of the clock, every breath Peter took, every sound the children made. What would happen now?

*An early example of Jews being singled out for humiliation. This photograph was taken in Cuxhaven in 1933. The couple are an **Aryan** woman and a Jewish man. The crime they committed, outlined on the placards they are wearing around their necks, was to get married to each other.*

CHAPTER 4

For or Against Hitler?

LOCAL PARTY GOVERNMENT

The Nazis were fanatical about conformity – people believing what they were told to believe, doing as they were told. They did not want any opposition – not even on a small scale. They liked things to be organized and regimented. So, Party members were given various jobs on a local level to make sure that everyone was behaving properly.

It was not just the *Blockwart* who was responsible for reporting on how people behaved – it was seen as the duty of every citizen to report anything suspicious that his neighbours might do or say. Indeed, the Hitler Youth movement taught children that their first duty was to the state – if their parents behaved in a suspect way then the children should report them. Many children did just this. Everyone soon learned to be careful what they said, all the time.

I was sitting in the garden, mending clothes, when *Herr* Neisse came to trim back the vine which was scrambling all over our little house. His rickety old cart, loaded with ladders and tools, stopped outside our gate, the gate bell rang, and he greeted me from across the hedge. If it had been a Sunday, or one of the many Party collection days, the voice would have been sharp and the greeting '*Heil Hitler*', for *Herr* Neisse was our gardener and our *Blockwart*, the Party representative for our neighbourhood. Besides pruning trees, mowing lawns and sweeping leaves he also collected Party subscriptions, sold postcards, pamphlets and so on to collect money for Party funds under the newly-launched 'Winter Help' campaign. He also sent reports on our behaviour to Party Headquarters: who had refused to hang out their flags and when, or how much and how willingly we had all given to Party funds.

On weekdays *Herr* Neisse was friendly, gentle, even a little shy. He had real concern for the trees, shrubs and plants in the gardens under his care. On Sundays things looked differently. **Resplendent** in his brown uniform, with shining boots and pill-box hat, his moustache trimmed to a neat rectangle, his left thumb hitched in his belt and his right arm raised in a rigid salute – he was a symbol of the spirit of the Nazi State. He was also one of the few cogs in the Nazi wheel that I knew at all well, for we shared the garden. When he worked there, his jacket carefully folded, his tools carefully sharpened and oiled, he seemed the very picture of a dedicated gardener, bringing on a vine here, discussing the soil. He even told me his life story as he worked. He was the son of a Saxon peasant, from whom he had inherited his accent and manner. He had fought in the First World War and returned to the chaos of Berlin a trifle surprised, as he admitted, by the suddenness and completeness of Germany's defeat. 'You see, *Frau Dr*, we seemed to be doing all right, we were told there had been great victories then suddenly, *Schluss*, finish, the Government at home sued for peace – they got their peace, and serve them damn well right, I say! I came back to Berlin because my Hilde lived here and I had promised her I would come back. She was waiting, my Hilde, bless her, she was waiting.' She must have been a great girl, his Hilde, for she then had to wait another ten years while he made enough money to marry her.

Herr Neisse was not sure who to blame for the loss of the First World War, but there was no doubt in his mind that the disaster which befell him so unreasonably in 1923 was the result of some dire plot. His savings, Hilde's savings, their plot of land, their humble enough hopes, had vanished into thin air overnight. 'The inflation, *Frau Dr*; suddenly we had one cup and saucer, which I gave to Hilde instead of a wedding certificate – funny, isn't it, how keen I was on the saucer?' Not funny, really, for when he spoke of this his voice and his hands shook badly. The loss of his money had shattered his faith in the Government.

Unemployment followed on the heels of inflation. The owners of the big houses could not afford a gardener. Then they moved away and were replaced by Jews. *Herr* Neisse had never liked Jews, or anyone who kept a shop – 'white Jews' he called them. But he still worked for them, saved carefully and finally married his Hilde. For two years they worked hard; they would soon be able to afford a half share in a vegetable stall. Then came 1929 and the American **depression**, which hit the newly recovering German economy hard. *Herr* Neisse was unemployed again and would have starved but for his **allotment**.

It was now that he began to attend the meeting of the National Socialist Party. The huge hall, filled with flags, the singing of the National Anthem, the speeches that put into words the hostility that he felt. The dishonour of the Treaty of Versailles, the need for a rebirth, the hunt for a scapegoat and finding one in the Jews. 'Not any one Jew, *Frau Dr*,' he would say. 'International Jewry.' He did not actually join the Party until 1931, mainly because Hilde thought it was silly. But he did join, in the end.

In 1933 *Herr* Neisse was rewarded for his **fidelity** to the Party by the post of *Blockwart*. He found it difficult to explain the **inconsistencies** of the policies of his Party, sometimes. Especially when all the Jews left Berlin-Dahlem and the high up Party officials moved in in great style, while Neisse still lived as he always had. But he felt sure of one thing – Hitler knew nothing of the bad things that were going on; Hitler would see things came all right in the end. *Herr* Neisse felt at home with Hitler, who had been a soldier, like him. 'He loves children, *Frau Dr*, and dogs too.'

These children are playing with building bricks made out of German deutschmarks (DM). This is real money, tied with string. The string was probably worth more than the money at the time. The photograph was taken in 1923. At this time one American dollar was worth about 4.2 million DM. In 1922 a loaf of bread cost 163 DM. In September 1923 a similar sized loaf cost 1,500,000 DM. Most people abandoned money altogether, and swapped things instead.

Familienbildnis, painted by Wolfgang Willrich in the 1930s. It shows an ideal Nazi family. They are simple people, farmers, or, at the least, people who appreciate the need to work the soil. They are not dangerous intellectuals, who read or think. They have four children already, and will probably have more. They obviously believe in family values, for the husband is there, involved with his family. The wife would not go out to work. She would obey her husband, and they would both obey the state.

WORKING WOMEN?

Before Hitler came to power, women had been going out of the home to work more and more. This was not acceptable to the Nazis. Women were supposed to get married and stay at home raising children. The children and the home **were** their work. The Nazis were not dismissive of these roles – they placed a great value on them.

Working women were acceptable only if they were single or widowed with no family. They were considered to be less fortunate than their married 'sisters'.
The Nazis were so keen on marriage and children because they wanted to breed a lot of 'racially pure' people to fill the Greater Germany they intended to create by conquering most of Europe. 'Racially pure' people were called Aryans, people who had German ancestors, rather than relatives from another race.

On the afternoon that *Herr* Neisse called to prune the vine I did not feel like talking. The war was barely a fortnight old. No one had imagined the German Army could have advanced into Poland at such dynamic speed. The Polish Air Force seemed to be grounded and the Poles were, with incredible bravery, charging the German tanks with their cavalry. The **Allies** seemed to do nothing. I don't know quite what I wanted them to do – but I was stunned that they did not act.

I had another reason for feeling deflated, too. I had decided to make a gesture – to join the **Red Cross**. I had decided that I would give three or four half days a week to rolling bandages, packing parcels, whatever it was they did. I turned up at the offices of the Red Cross feeling, I must admit, **virtuous**. I was not going to let the fact that my country was at war with Germany interfere with my conviction that all human life was important. I was greeted by a weary looking blonde whose blue eyes changed from friendly enquiry to frank bewilderment on hearing my offer. I was married? Yes. I had children? Yes. Then how, if she might ask, had I imagined I could join the Red Cross?

It was my turn to look bewildered. Was there no room for voluntary help? 'None whatsoever,' she said firmly. 'Go back to your home and your children, *Frau* Bielenberg, that is where you belong.' She looked so tired that I remarked on it, and she replied that she had more work than she could really handle. But for all this, I was not to be allowed to join. I had to stay in my kitchen, with my children.

It was now that *Herr* Neisse chose to talk about the war, pitying me, a stranger 'in a foreign land'. I tried to stay composed and replied that Germany was now my home, but that I tried to think of the war as little as possible. Poor Neisse, he had his problems with the war, too. He, like many Germans, had a collection of patriotic postcards which he had shown me. One of them showed a lurid scene of starving women and children being threatened by Jews with whips. This, the caption had said, showed a Russian **concentration camp**. But now Russia was our ally. The postcard was withdrawn, then re-issued with a caption saying it was of British concentration camps in South Africa. This was hard to explain, but he did not want to lose faith in the Party. Poor bloke, **sold down the river** again.

The ideal Nazi family was not just a subject for paintings. Many people actually tried to achieve it. A wife and a clutch of children, preferably with the Aryan blonde hair and blue eyes, were an asset to any member of the Government. Wives, of course, had to be carefully chosen to be capable of having children and bringing them up 'properly'. This was most important in the case of people that the Government had to rely on completely. Members of the SS, for instance, had to send the women they wanted to marry for several interviews (to establish their political views and racial purity) and medical examinations (to see if they were capable of having children). If they passed these tests then they were sent to special Bräuteschule – bride schools, where they were rigorously trained in the skills of motherhood.

German rations, 5 October, 1939.
A week's food was:

- 350g   *of bread*
- 7g   *of jam*
- 35g   *of fat (butter, lard or bacon)*
    – if obtainable
- 35g   *of sugar*
- 35g   *of meat – if obtainable*
- 3.5g   *of coffee*

German rations, like those in Britain, varied over the years. The 1939 ration was a generous one compared to the ration in 1945.

People in the country and those with gardens and allotments in the towns could grow food, even keep animals for meat and eggs. People living in towns and cities, with no scope to grow their own food, had to rely on friends, queueing and the black market. The black market was the name given to selling things illegally. The black market sold food, clothes, cigarettes, almost everything. As it was illegal, it was dangerous to sell or buy things on the black market. The penalty was prison or execution.

As *Herr* Neisse left that day he met my son Nicky coming home from school. They stopped on the corner and talked, then Nicky came skipping up the road towards me. 'I went home with Werner first,' he said. 'Do you know Mummy, Werner says his mum listens to the radio, just the way you do, with your ear right up against it.' For a moment I held my breath. She must have been listening to foreign radio, like I did, for which there was now a minimum punishment of five years in prison and a maximum penalty of death. I had never met Werner's mother, but now we were as bound to each other as if we had committed a murder together. 'She's probably deaf as a post, just like me,' I said firmly.

So not everyone was for Hitler, yet you could never know. There were other things to occupy the mind, in any case. On market days I had to be up very early indeed for, as soon as food **rationing** was introduced everything that was not on ration cards vanished from shop windows overnight. Unless you knew a shopkeeper well, or better still a farmer, you could hardly get a thing to eat. Not only did I have no contacts like this, we also had very little money. This seemed an adventure at first, the children and I travelled all over Berlin looking for a shop or stall that was a few *pfennigs* cheaper. Then Peter pointed out we spent more on bus fares than we saved. We stuck to places we could walk to.

The glamour of being poor soon wore off in the tedium of queueing. One morning I had set the alarm for 5 a.m., but had not set out until late, for various things had delayed me. I passed no one on the road and imagined everyone else at home already, wondering where I had been. It was hardly worth going, but I went on, thinking as I went about the war, which was now in its sixth week. As I wandered past Nicky's kindergarten I though about all the children inside, being taught about the **master race**, and hoped, desperately, that they would soon be being taught something different.

I was amazed when I reached the market. What had happened to the stalls? There shouldn't have been a cabbage stalk left, but the stalls were still half full, there were very few queues, most people were standing around chatting in groups. I waited at the baker's stall. His wife clipped my **coupons** and recklessly shoved an extra loaf into my bag. 'We won't be needing these much longer, *Frau Dr*, peace **negotiations** are going on this very minute!' 'It's true,' cried *Frau* Smidt from the vegetable stall. We were all beside ourselves with joy, and the local policeman confirmed it. I hurried home and phoned Peter. He had heard rumours, nothing more, he would get in touch. The radio news said nothing of peace. When Peter returned it turned out to have been a **propaganda** exercise by the British Government, to test German morale.

The war went on. So did rationing. Winter set in. We managed to get hold of some rabbits and chickens to keep, but were not good with livestock. One morning, when we went to feed the rabbits four furry rigid stones dropped to the ground from the hutch – they had frozen. The hens, which lived in the cellar, did not meet with much local approval – ours was considered too good a district to be used like allotments. Indeed, we were seen as pretty suspect all round. But we did have friends, like-minded friends, who did call round often. I had no maid and I could **disconnect** my telephone. These were priceless advantages to plotters, and that is what we were. I did not take part in the discussion much. I did not really know enough, and I had to keep the boys out of the way. Then, in January, 1940, Peter was called up. He was back within four weeks, a friend managed to get him back, but we suddenly realized it could happen again, at any time. Then the impossible happened. France fell in just six short weeks. Suddenly it seemed that Hitler would have his thousand year Reich after all, well beyond our lifetimes. We felt hopeless and helpless. So, because someone happened to have got hold of a load of **crayfish**, while someone else had hold of some **aquavit**, because Adam and Clarita had got married and were moving into a flat near us, because everything was so awful, someone suggested that we should give a party. So we did.

SCHOOLS

The Nazis knew the value of propaganda and they knew the value of getting children to accept their ways early on, so that they would be less likely to question them. From as early as 1934, children were taught the Nazi view of history, the Nazi view of race, the Nazi view of everything. They were taught the Nazi salute and learned their lessons under Nazi flags and the regulation painting of Hitler.

School timetables show that the children were taught sport, Geography, History, Race Studies, Singing, Maths, Domestic Science for the girls and 'military studies' for the boys and Ideology. All these, even the less propaganda-sounding of them, were presented in the 'right' light – Geography stressed the 'proper borders for Germany'. History taught the shamefulness of the Treaty of Versailles and the borders it had imposed on Germany. Domestic Science stressed motherhood as the only goal for women. Singing concentrated on marching songs and songs that had the 'right' message.

We ate the crayfish and drank the aquavit in a small group first, before the larger party took place. We all knew each other very well by now, and trusted each other enough to get quite drunk. We were still stunned by events in France, and not quite ourselves. The table was cleared, more friends appeared with more bottles and then one of our friends came in, having borrowed one of Peter's brown shirts and a black tie, corked his upper lip and pulled his hair forward in exact imitation of Hitler's forelock. This set everyone off into reckless imitations and speeches. We nearly forgot the time, the date, the sheer awfulness of it all. We even tuned the radio into band music from England, loud enough to be heard. But, for all the drink, for all the seeming lack of caution, there were still always four of the men **patrolling** the garden at all times, just in case.

Our first acquaintance with the neighbours was a dispute over the chickens, which was unfortunate. But, very gradually we got to know them, discovered **mutual** friends and were eventually invited to dinner. All the same they were new people and everyone would be cautious. We were none of us Nazis, we could be pretty sure of that. But were we all, drunk or sober, also discreet? Peter and Dr Carl Langbehn got on really well. They had discovered ancestors from the same part of Germany, and I could see that, despite the difference in age, they had a similar outlook. I found myself keeping one ear on their conversation and soon realized that the same was true of Carl's mother, *Frau* Langbehn. When Peter made a rather unguarded remark she relaxed and said, 'I live in fear that Carl will say too much. Our phone has been tapped and so on...' Langbehn then told us about the time he met **Himmler** and was asked to stay to tea and dinner. 'It was awful,' said *Frau* Langbehn. 'I had to talk to his wife while hearing Carl tell Himmler of cases where the SS had brought people in to question them and the next thing anyone knew their ashes were sent home to their wives. He is always pushing the boundaries to see how far he can go in criticizing the Government.' We talked about the SS, the Government in general. Then Langbehn said that he was sure that it was Hitler who was the key figure. 'Get rid of him and they'll all be at each other's throats,' he said. I found myself shivering, imagining the worry his mother had, for it was clear he was very close to speaking his mind even more openly than he had so far.

Peter and I walked on for a while, when we left the dinner, rather than going straight home. We wanted to walk and talk alone. The funny thing was that in Germany life went on as normal in some ways, people fell in love, dinner was cooked, children cared for, yet sudden jolts, like the invasion of France and the talk of the SS at dinner, brought home the truth of the **iniquitous** core – one man's desire to dominate, to have power over all his fellow men.

Now the British began to bomb Berlin. Happy as I was in one way, it was no use pretending that I was not scared stiff when night after night, just about bedtime, the haunting wail of the **sirens** sent me hustling down to the cellar where, for several hours, I would sit wrapped in a rug, trying to amuse the children among the buckets, dish-cloths, **stirrup pumps** and hens. By this time Peter had stopped believing that the Government could be overthrown. He had left the Civil Service and had not yet been called up. His firm sent him to Norway. We were to move to Austria to get away from the bombing. We moved and the children caught whooping cough at the same time – we were not made very welcome on our arrival. Even when the children stopped whooping we did not seem to fit in. Peter was able to arrange for me to visit him in Norway, though the children had to stay behind. I went, but wished I hadn't on my return – the 'reliable' friend who had had the children had neglected them and then, almost at once, I had to leave them again to go into hospital. Peter came to see me and we decided that the children and I would return to Berlin.

A French city, bombed by the Germans, being watched over by a German soldier (the shadow in the foreground on the left). The German Army was able to take France over so quickly partly because the French were taken by surprise, partly by sheer numbers and organization, but also because they went in hard and fast with total ruthlessness and disregard for lives or property.

CHAPTER 5

A Dilemma

In 1942, just after the fall of Stalingrad, a full year after Hitler had **decreed** that all the Jews living in Germany must have the **Star of David** and the word 'Jew' sewn on their coats, before the SS decision to purify Germany of Jews, I was put in a moral dilemma. Some Jews, called 'submarines', removed their stars and went into hiding. They disappeared, surfacing here, there and everywhere – anywhere where they might find a hiding place. They had no ration cards. Every week a friend of mine, Ilse Liedke, collected spare coupons for them. One morning she had a blonde woman with her when she called, who would not come into the house. Having checked that the phone was unplugged, Ilse explained why. The woman was a Jew. When the Gestapo came hammering at the door of her flat she and her husband had removed their stars and escaped down the fire escape. They had been living in attics and cellars ever since. They had got her hair dyed at a hairdressers, she could pass as Aryan, but her husband was so unmistakably Jewish that he had to stay hidden all the time.

They had been hiding with a Catholic priest nearby, but people were suspicious, he was sure they had said something, his house was being watched. He had not asked the Jews to go, but it would be safer if they did. Could they come to me? I thought about the neighbours, many of whom were great supporters of Hitler. But whether I liked it or not, prepared or unprepared, the moment had come. I asked the woman in. She sat on the sofa next to me, her head bent, twisting her wedding ring round and round. They could not go to Ilse. She was half Jewish, so suspect. They could not stay with the priest. I was trying, while talking and watching her twisting fingers, to work out how I could have them in the house. We now had a maid. I would have to send her on holiday. We had a cellar they could stay in. But I, too, was a suspect person, being English. Carl Langbehn had vouched for my good behaviour while Peter was away. I would have to ask him. I told her she could stay with me in the house all day, but that I would have to ask Carl, could not promise anything, until that night. Even so, she was so grateful. As soon as the maid was gone the woman went around the house polishing, scrubbing and sweeping. We played snakes and ladders with the children and she helped me cook supper and get them to bed. Then I slipped next door to talk to Carl. I knew he helped Jews himself, I did not expect any difficulty. He said I should send them away. I was English, suspected, Nicky was at school and might so easily say something. We would all be caught. Then they, I and Peter would be off to a concentration camp. I could not tell them to go at once. I said they could stay at least for one night. They left the next night. They left a shining house and a note thanking me for just two miserable days grace. I never saw the man, but he must have been nice, the woman spoke of him with such affection.

Hinaus mit   allen Störenfrieden!

A poster from 1933 showing the Hitler Youth scattering 'undesirable' Jews. From the beginning, Hitler was rabidly anti-Jewish. By 1942, when Christabel Bielenberg faced her dilemma, Jews were already being herded into concentration camps and the 'final solution' to the 'Jewish problem' – killing them all – had begun.

Einheit der Jugend in der Hitlerjugend!

CHAPTER 6

Leaving Berlin

In the summer of 1943 we decided that the children should not go through another winter in Berlin. Our third son, Christopher, had been born there in 1942 and, despite the black market, the food situation got worse month by month. We also knew that longer nights would bring renewed British bombing raids. Also, by 1943, Peter saw his luck could not last forever. He had been called up in the spring. Carl Langbehn had managed to get him transferred to an aircraft factory in West Prussia, but sooner or later he would have to go to the front.

We decided to go to Rohrbach, in the Black Forest. We arrived there in September on board a tiny train, which had some difficulty in getting up the **incline**, but finally puffed to a stop beside a small weather-worn yellow house. We were left standing on the platform (just a piece of raised ground) with an assortment of packages around us, mostly tied with rope. The arrival of the train had obviously disturbed the stationmaster at his haymaking. His red cap was impressive, but the rest of him was covered in hayseeds and a long rake was propped up on the wall. He told us that Rohrbach was only a few kilometres up the valley, we could get a lift there with the milk cart. We would have to ride with the empty cans but there would be room for us too. We had not long to wait before a small wooden cart, pulled by a fat chestnut horse, arrived. A large fellow climbed down, put some water into a fire bucket for the horse and set about unloading the cans. Although there were only five of them, it took a while – he and the stationmaster had a lot to talk about!

Hans Bausch was the milkman's name. He was very friendly and willingly loaded us onto the cart. He even let Nicky drive the cart for some of the way. We reached the village and passed through it, headed for our new home, where we hoped to spend the rest of the war. As we passed a schoolhouse, John, his eye catching the blackboard through the window, asked, 'Will I have to go to that school?' 'Yes, I expect so.' 'Why?' Suddenly I was so despondent. Why indeed? I should have been glad to have been coming somewhere friendly, quiet, peaceful. I was so much better off than so many other people in Germany. I knew this. I also knew that I was tired of the nomadic life, so inevitable for **evacuees**. I was tired of living in spare bedrooms, apologising for my children, scrounging for my children, trying to fight the urge to go home. I had given in to that urge when in Austria, only to find that 'home' in Berlin was now a frail fortress on the front line. It seemed to me that Rohrbach would be just another temporary hiding place, miserable like all of the others. The more I thought about it the more miserable I became. By the time we reached our new home the sun had gone down and the air was cold. The farmhouse we had come to was by far the most **dilapidated** of all those we had passed. My heart sank.

Peter's aunt, Ulla, who helped us over and over again in our drifting state, came out of the farmhouse to meet us. I could tell from the look on her face that all was not well. The rooms that we had rented, paid for in advance, had been given to other **refugees**. We were expected to sleep in a couple of filthy attics. The farm itself was so poor that it could barely feed the owners, let alone the other 'guests'. Worst of all the farm's owner was one of the few Nazis in the valley. We would have to leave as soon as possible.

The following day we made a despairing approach to the innkeeper of the *Gasthaus Adler*, the only inn in the village, and *Frau* Muckle agreed to feed and house us. She let us have the room next to the sitting room to live in and moved out of her bedroom, which was above this room and joined to it by a small wooden staircase, so that I could sleep there. She even found two small bedrooms for the boys. Ulla found a room nearby, in the house of the priest's housekeeper. I soon discovered that pleasure is all a matter of comparison. Our new home was far from luxurious, but there were no creaking shutters, no watching, no suits of creaking armour (as in one place we had stayed at) – our newest refuge had a view down the valley and a door to the street, chairs, a table, a sofa, even a **spinet**. It also had a green tiled stove in one corner. It was a comparative heaven.

While the Nazi State could not dominate the countryside as effectively as it controlled places like Berlin, it still affected the way people behaved. The banner hung between the trees has yet another anti-Jewish slogan on it. However, the extent of Nazi influence was much more dependent on the politics of the local administrators.

CHAPTER 7

Rohrbach

I soon got used to telling the time of day by the thin chime from the church steeple that called the villagers to prayer, or by the jingle of the bells around the necks of the cows going to the pasture in the morning and back in the evening, all set to produce a jugful or so of milk from their diet of moss and weeds. I even got used to the smell of *gille*, the cow-house smell that crept up through the floorboards and filled every corner of the house. I decided that the inn was a good place for the likes of me, fond of a good gossip. The beer might be thin, the wine non-existent, but every Sunday after **mass**, and on some evenings too, the villagers gathered in the parlour. As they chatted and I came to understand their **dialect**, I put names to faces and people to houses.

The baker from the lower part of the village was also mayor, managing to run the village, in these troubled times, as carefully as he could. You had to watch what you said to the other baker; his bread was bad too. The mayor's clerk, Sepp Kern, was the local **cobbler**; his wife kept a shop in the village. He and the mayor, their day's work done, met in the mayor's office and conducted the village business. Kern sat under the regulation picture of the Führer and typed up ration cards, wood chopping permits, birth and death certificates, the whole record of life in the village. When I knew him better I asked what he thought about the war. He was a large kindly man, but very shrewd and careful how he voiced his opinions. He eventually eyed me over his steel-rimmed spectacles and said, 'The way I see it, *Frau Dr*, I don't think that pile of shoes I have to mend will get any smaller, whoever wins the war.'

There was the village gossip, who knew the scandal almost before it had happened, the churchwarden, who was also the local vet and the sad-eyed priest who taught at the village school. But the most important figure in my life was *Frau* Muckle, a sturdy little widow with thinning black hair and shrewd brown eyes. Despite the need to be careful, she soon betrayed her scorn for the Nazis and all their works. She fed us and cared for us as well as she could and became a good friend. She came from the lowlands and planned, as soon as her son Ernst came back from the war, to move back there with him and his wife. Until then she ruled the inn with a **thrifty** hand and a warm heart, alternately bullying and mothering her only help, Martina. Martina was up by six every morning. She lit the stove, fed the animals, mucked out the cow house, worked in the fields – she was constantly on the go, apart from the times when *Frau* Muckle sat her down and fed her potato soup, or bacon and buttermilk. Rohrbach was our little world, an unimportant world, with no say in the affairs of state, but it still had to carry the burden of Hitler's dreams of conquest. There were no young men in the village or the farmhouses up and down the valley. The back page of the local paper had lists of sons who would never come back to turn the soil or wield an axe again.

VILLAGES

Rohrbach managed to stay relatively unaffected by the Nazis. It was small, it was in the extreme west of Germany, it had a mayor who was not Nazi. Some villages, especially in central Germany, were changed far more.

A study of Körle, about 150 km from Berlin (compared to Rohrbach's 350 km), shows that the village was, from 1933 onwards, controlled by a Nazi mayor. The villagers were forced into an 'ideological co-ordination' – making everyone think the same. Nazi propaganda stressed family life – but in fact they liked life to concentrate on their various groups. So the groups took over and weakened family life. Families were divided when members disagreed about the Nazis. Not everyone in the village supported the Nazis. Older people were less quick to conform. They hid food from officials; towards the end of the war some villagers even hid soldiers who were **deserting** from the army.

I went back to Berlin just before winter came. I heard that Carl had been arrested. He had gone to the Gestapo headquarters in Prinz Albrechtstrasse to plead for a prisoner once too often. Our old home was now just a house with walls; I knew I had once lived there, but had no urge to return. While I was there we were bombed three times. The bombs fell on Nazis and anti-Nazis, on women and children, works of art, dogs and pet canaries. They were **wanton** and quite, quite impersonal. Before he was arrested Carl had dug an air-raid shelter. His mother and I cowered in it, while pieces of **shrapnel** bounced off the roof. She would not leave Berlin. I could not wait to.

The snows came to Rohrbach in November, billowing up the valley and piling up against doors and windows. And although there were storms, powercuts and other troubles, it was safe. *Frau* Muckle would do her rounds to lock up each night, and bid us goodnight. I was so grateful for all that she had done for us.

PROPAGANDA

People in Nazi German were bombarded with propaganda from all sides. Posters, banners with slogans, flags and paintings of Hitler hung everywhere – these were all forms of visual propaganda. People also heard propaganda constantly on the radio, at rallies and at Party meetings.

The man behind all this was Joseph Goebbels, who joined the Nazi Party in 1922 and was made Minister of Enlightenment and Propaganda in 1933. He censored everything in the newspapers, on the radio, in books, even art and music, to make sure that they were 'politically correct' – in line with Nazi ideas. Schools had to teach 'facts' that were also heavily censored. His plan was to fill every corner of everyday life with propaganda and so dominate everyone's lives.

This poster of a man digging his garden has the slogan 'Strength through Joy'. This was a common slogan and was associated with the Nazi campaign to try to get people to use their leisure time 'properly'. This usually involved group activities, most of them of a healthy, outdoor nature. The Nazis ran Strength through Joy cruises, rallies, concerts, camping trips and so on. These events usually involved people from the towns and cities, or in the case of things like cruises, people who had done something for the Party that merited reward.

A photograph of Staff Sergeant F. T. Lusic, getting ready to fly off in his plane which he nicknamed 'Meat Hound'. Lusic was an air gunner. His plane was a B-17 Flying Fortress, part of the 8th Army Air Force. The photo was taken on 4 May, 1943. The ammunition for his machine gun is slung round his neck.

In the summer of 1944, I was laying the table for lunch when Hans Bausch's head appeared at the window. He looked excited. '*Frau Dr*, I have something for you.' 'Yes Hans, what?' 'An American, *Frau Dr*, tall with dark curly hair. He's wearing overalls with pockets in the knees and his boots are the softest leather, lined with fur.' 'Where did you find him, Hans?' 'Up in the woods, lying against my woodpile.' 'Where is he now?' 'Asleep in my kitchen.' I asked *Frau* Muckle to make lunch a little late and followed Hans up the road and along the winding track to his house. He lifted the latch, opened the door and stood back to let me go in. There, stretched out on a narrow bench against the far wall, was a tall young man in blue airman's overalls. He had taken off his fur-lined boots and was using them as a pillow. As I looked down at him I realized that Germany had lost the war. It was not his face that convinced me, but his general air of health and vitality, the sheer quality of his clothes and equipment. Suddenly I felt shabby, old, dilapidated and defeated.

'Hi,' I said, shaking him. 'Hi, beautiful,' he said without even opening his eyes, then sat up suddenly, very wide awake. 'My name's Chris Bielenberg and I have just been told by our milkman that he found you propping up his woodpile.' 'I guess that's just about it, Ma'am,' he replied with a faint smile. 'I'm sure glad to see you. I guess I'd been walking for a long time. Two days and two nights, maybe, heading west. We got shot up and baled out over some little town. When I got this far I realized I was going to have to give myself up, so I surrendered to this guy, but he just brought me here.' 'What bothers me,' I said 'is what to do with you.' 'It's no problem, Ma'am,' he said. 'I guess the war is over for me now.' It was only then, hearing the sudden flatness in his voice, that I realized how exhausted he must be.

'I think you had better give in,' I said. 'Your only chance otherwise would be to try to get to Switzerland, and that would mean crossing the Rhine.' 'The Rhine, Ma'am, what's that?' he asked. I was stunned. 'Well, it's a big river,' I said, 'but never mind – tell me about England, how are they doing?' He looked suddenly wary, his answer was non-committal. 'England is a pretty little country, full of cute fields and nice flowers.' 'I know, but what about the war?' 'The war? The war, Ma'am, is in the bag, but why ask all these questions?'

'You're sure you want to give yourself up?' 'Yes.' 'OK, sit down and rest and I'll fetch the mayor.' The mayor looked very serious when I told him the news. I answered his questions patiently. Yes, I was sure he was an American. No, I didn't know what to do, but phoning the police seemed to be the only sensible option. So he and Sepp Kern, the clerk, set off to phone from Sepp's wife's shop. I trooped after them. The shop was cleared and the phone call made. At first he tried the town of Donaueschingen, but there was a raid on; we could not get through. So he tried Furtwangen, only to find that it took a long time for the report to be taken seriously. But at last he was told that he was believed, but that, at least temporarily, we would have to cope with the airman ourselves, another air-raid was imminent and everyone was busy. 'We'll have to lock him up in the cell,' said the mayor. 'The cell! It's been at least five years since anyone was in there, I don't even know where the key is...' 'Orders are orders, Sepp, we will have to find the key or break the door down.' Sepp found the key and off we trooped to the cell. I had never before heard of this cell, although most villages had one. It was mostly used, in the old days, to lock up rowdy drunks until they cooled down. It was, in fact, the small room with the rusty door next to the schoolhouse. I had always assumed it was the coalhouse. The key was so rusty that it needed a lot of oil and the blacksmith with an iron bar to get the cell open. It was small, bare and filthy. So *Frau* Muckle and I were ordered to feed the airman while the cell was made 'respectable'. We went to *Frau* Muckle's, all of us. The airman refused to answer any questions, but I persuaded him at least to give his name and **number**. *Frau* Muckle had made a banquet of roast pork and mashed potatoes, with dumplings covered with caramelized sugar to follow.

The American was obviously ravenously hungry and we watched a week's ration disappear at a sitting. The unaccustomed wine made everyone more relaxed, so we got through the time until the cell was ready. As we turned to go the airman noticed a bust of Abraham Lincoln on the mantlepiece. I could see, from his expression that this would be the **punchline** of tales told later to his grandchildren. He was taken to his cell which now had a strip of carpet, a mattress on the bench and clean sheets on the mattress. He was locked in. Then we realized we had to take his papers, so we unlocked the door and took his things away. He had identity papers, a map of south-west Germany, a photograph of a girl and some English money. He was not armed. We gave him the photo back but put the other things by. The next morning two badly uniformed guards arrived. Refreshed and invigorated, towering above his captors, our airman strode off; his guards had to break into little runs to keep up with him. The village settled down again to the business of getting the hay in.

AMERICA JOINS THE WAR

The Americans had tried to keep out of the war. They helped Britain and the Allies from the beginning by sending war supplies (at a price). Later they sent food too. But they would not commit themselves to fight, even when France fell to the Germans. Then, in December, 1941, the Japanese (allies of the Germans) bombed the American Fleet at Pearl Harbor. America declared war on Japan and Germany.

When the Americans entered the war most of the rest of Europe had been fighting for about three years. The Americans arrived fresh to the war, well fed, well equipped and well trained. When news came that America had joined the war, Winston Churchill, the British Prime Minister, is said to have remarked, 'So we have won after all.'

CHAPTER 8

The July Plot and After

THE JULY PLOT

The plan of the July Plot was to plant a time bomb in Hitler's military headquarters in East Prussia, timed to go off during one of his meetings. The army generals in the plot would then take over and put the civilians who were in the plot in power. These people would then declare an armistice at once. The bomb was planted by Colonel von Staffenberg. He left just before it exploded. The blast was a strong one and he assumed it had done its work. A new, non-Nazi government was declared.

But Hitler had chosen to hold his meeting in an upstairs room, not in the underground bunker where the meetings were usually held. Staffenberg and other conspirators who could be found were shot at once. Others, caught later, were put on trial (see caption on page 29). Hitler had had a miraculous escape. The shock affected him badly. He became more and more neurotic and suspicious.

Then, in July, news came on the radio that there had been an attempt to blow up Hitler. But the plot had failed, a list of generals involved was read; the only one that rang a bell was Staffenberg; but he rang a very big bell indeed. Yet, even then, I could hope that no one I knew and loved was involved. The post had just come in, with a letter to Aunt Ulla from Peter. The letter asked her to look after us. It was as if my heart stopped beating, as if I was held rigid in a cold, inflexible vice.

Some days after the first radio announcement, a week perhaps, they published a first list of 'conspirators'. They were all army officers, some of whom I had known. Peter was not on the list, but there was no news from him, either. Then, on 8 August a postcard came, unsigned. It read 'Adam arrested, can't think why, love to all.' Then nothing. I sent three letters to Peter begging him to write and a telegram asking for money. I wrote to his boss. No reply. A list of the main 'civilian' conspirators was published: those who would have run the country if Hitler had died. Adam's name was on the list. They were to be hanged.

There was no comfort anywhere and no news from Peter. One day I got back from mushrooming to find Nicky doing his homework and a letter for me from Berlin. It was from a friend there, Mabel Horbottle. It said, 'Dear Chris, I do not like having to be the one to give you this news. Peter was arrested in Graudenz on 6 August. We naturally feel certain that he will soon be out again and send you our love. We will let you know as soon as we have further news.' Nicky's pen scratched on the paper, the old wooden clock on the wall ticked off the seconds. I do not know how long I sat there, but suddenly I was not alone, Ulla was there reading it over my shoulder. She began to sob. 'Oh, no, Chris, no,' she sobbed. 'First my Albrecht and now Peter, oh no, oh my God, no.' I realized that Nicky had stopped writing and was staring at me over her head. I got her upstairs to my bed, found her an aspirin, got it down her and sat holding her hand until she fell asleep. Then I went downstairs. At first I could not see Nicky. His head was buried in his arms, his face was wizened and he was sobbing dry, convulsive sobs. 'Is Daddy dead?' he asked. 'No, but he is in prison.' 'Why?' 'Because an enemy in Graudenz has made false accusations about him.' 'But the police will stop this, won't they?' 'Well, yes,' I said feebly. He did not believe me. Every line of his body told me so. Then he said, 'When the war is over I don't want to stay here. I want to go to England and be English. In England the police don't let you be put in prison for things you haven't done.' We stood, hand in hand, looking out of the window until it was time for him to go and help Martina fetch the cows. That night, alone in the parlour, I listened to the English news. They were advancing. How fast could they go? They must know it was important to reach Berlin before the Russians. I suddenly knew that I had to go to Munich and then to Berlin.

I went first to Munich, to the *Bankhaus* Seiler. I asked why Peter was in prison, why I had not been told. *Herr* Seiler said he had had no time to let me know yet – I probably knew why better than he did, he said. He then said that he knew five of the arrested men and had no sympathy for any of them, but he would testify for two of them; which two he did not know. He asked if Peter had known any of the conspirators, when I mentioned Adam he said that Adam had been hanged. I caught the next train for Berlin. I was amazed at the sight of Berlin – there had been so much bombing that it was hardly recognisable. I made my way, through the air raids that seemed non-stop, to my house, where Mabel and her husband, Arnold, and I discussed Peter's situation. Arnold seemed to think Peter was safe enough where he was, I desperately wanted him to try to get Peter out, or at least moved. I spent five days in Berlin, then went home. On the way I went to see an SS officer who we had known before the war. He said he would try hard to get Peter transferred. I thought he would keep his word, he sounded so sincere when he said it; but when I arrived back it was to find that an SS officer had been to our village. I was to be placed under house arrest. Sepp told me, in a very apologetic manner and added, 'If you want to go to Furtwanger or any place, to do some shopping, just let us know. I'll have John's shoes fixed for you tomorrow.'

Lieutenant General von Witzleben, one of the army officers involved in the July Plot, in uniform before the plot and at his trial. He was not allowed to have a belt, so had to hold his trousers up with his hands. One of the things that shocked Hitler's supporters most about the July Plot was the involvement of so many people who were high in Hitler's army or government. The trial of the eight army officers began on 8 August, 1944. The were hanged for the crime, by piano wire strung from meat hooks. After they were hanged a huge search was carried out to find others who may have been involved.

CHAPTER 9

Back to Berlin

On 24 December, 1944, I set off on a second journey to Berlin. I had been given permission by the Gestapo to visit Peter in Ravensbrück, a concentration camp, north of Berlin. I could only think of two reasons why they should do this. Arnold might have pulled all the strings he could and they could have agreed in a fit of curiosity to see what I was like; or it was to be a farewell visit before his execution. The latter was far more likely. I rose at 3 a.m. and looked in on the boys, who were sleeping soundly. We had celebrated Christmas a day early here, just in case. When I got downstairs *Frau* Muckle was frying bacon in a pan. She bustled around laying the table, trying to appear ordinary, yet she laid the best china and made the most extravagant breakfast possible. We both knew it was possible that she would never see me again.

Women clearing the rubble in Berlin after a bombing raid in 1945. All they had to work with were buckets, and they were nicknamed 'rubble women'. One of the most interesting things about this photograph is that it could equally well have been taken in England. Photographs of London, Coventry and other bombed English cities at the time show similar scenes, even down to the aprons.

I strode along to the station, feeling real relief to be doing something after weeks of worry. Only a couple of scribbled, censored notes had reached me from Peter, one to announce his removal to Berlin, the other his arrival at Ravensbrück. I decided to see how the land lay in Berlin, but I was almost sure that my best plan would be to ask to see *Kriminalrat* Lange, the chief interrogator. Sepp had told me the Germans believed that I had influential connections in England. I would play on that. The worst that could happen would be that I would be arrested too. I was held up in Tuttlingen, for it was here that I had to change for the Berlin Express. It seemed to be indefinitely delayed, so I wandered round the town. It was clean, neat and cheerful. No bomb craters here, anyway. I looked in the windows of the houses, trying to guess who lived in them by the sort of tree they had, but that made me feel lonely, so I made my way back to the station. My train arrived at last. I found a carriage where the windows were not broken. It was at the front, right behind the engine, a dangerous place to be if more bombers came over, but warm. I was asleep before the train even pulled out of the station.

I woke in Stuttgart. There seemed to have been a raid there; several houses were still burning. The carriage and the corridor were now overflowing with soldiers. I went to the toilet and found, when I got back, a woman asleep in my seat. I decided to sit in the corridor. There were soldiers playing cards and one Berliner telling everyone his part in the retreat from France. 'Run – run, I have never run so fast in all my life. Once an army gets running nothing can stop it. First we threw away our drinking bottles; then our helmets, belts and ammunition; then our rifles.' 'Where are you going to now?' I asked. 'I haven't a clue, but I know one thing, I'm not after an Iron Cross. I've got this far and at the end I want to be back in Berlin, with the missus, running my old vegetable stall.' I remembered that I had a bottle of **kirsch** in my bag, a whole litre. I had meant it as a present for Arnold, but I went and got it now. Someone produced a penknife, and got the cork out of the bottle, handing it back to me with a bow to have the first sip. We sat and sang and talked through the night. I was sorry to see them go at Magdeburg. They could have been a cross-section of any army anywhere. Blown about by the whims of those higher up, they had no real hates, resentments, even ambition, beyond getting home to their families alive. When they had gone I moved to the back of the train. Now we were nearer Berlin the danger of bombing was greater, so I preferred to move back, despite the cold. Every station we passed now was crowded with refugees; patient groups of old people, women and children, with their things in bundles and sacks around them. They all seemed to be trying to get south and west.

BOMBS

Bombing raids happened at night more often than in the day-time. This was the safest time for the bomber pilots. The Second World War was one of the first wars where the fighting was not just confined to the armies of both sides. In this war civilians were bombed too, by both sides.

Bombs came in different sizes. Ordinary bombs were shaped like big bullets. The pointed end of each bomb dug into the earth, then it blew up. These bombs usually weighed between 50 and 300 kg. Bigger bombs, used on land or at sea, called mines, were dropped by parachute. They were bigger and did not dig into the earth. They exploded as soon as they landed. Mines did a lot of damage. They could blow up a person from 400 m away, or toss a bus up in the air. Bombs did not have to be big to cause a lot of damage. For instance, firebombs only weighed about 1 kg. They were dropped in bundles, and started fires. Unless the fires were put out quickly a lot of damage could be done.

When I reached Berlin the gaunt grey city looked worse than ever. One of the soldiers had said to me on the train, 'If they want to hit more targets, they'll have to bring them with them.' I could see what he meant. I made my way home, where Mabel and Arnold were living now. They greeted me, and led me to my room. I dug out the parcels of butter, bread and bacon I had been able to bring, and felt a bit mean about the kirsch. The house had done quite well from the bombing. It had only been hit once but that, Arnold said, had been a nasty one with a delayed explosion. I had heard of these – particularly despicable bombs which had been devised to kill or maim anyone foolish enough to try to stop to rescue anything from the rubble. For some while we avoided the reason for my coming to Berlin at all. Then Arnold disconnected the telephone and began to speak. He was not happy about the fact that nothing definite seemed to be happening one way or the other. He had got Peter transferred, on my request, but was now worried because he was in the hands of expert interrogators, men who knew he had had friends who were involved in the July Plot and who wanted his confession to being involved too. 'I don't think they have anything on him, but I think they dislike him very much. He is too big, too good looking, too arrogant for them. Also he does not know Adam and Carl are dead (this was the first I knew of Carl's death) so he may be trying to protect them in some way. You can help. You have to be at Ravensbrück at ten o'clock the day after tomorrow. You must try to convey to him that they are dead. They cannot speak against him, nor do they need protection.' 'I'll do my best, Arnold.' was all I could say.

The next day there was nothing to do, so I decided to go to find an old friend of ours, Lexi. Mabel had said she was still living in the Budapesterstrasse, although she could not imagine where – the whole area around the Berlin zoo was even more devastated than any other part of Berlin. I crossed the road to avoid Carl's gate. I would have to face his mother, but I could not do so yet. I caught the bus into central Berlin. When we reached the Halensee, past the old ruins and the new ones, I decided I would get out and walk. Then I thought that, before seeing Lexi and, even more important, Peter, I might have my hair done. I could go to the hairdressers nearby that I had always gone to before. I walked along remembering *Fräulein* Lydia and her tales of her boyfriend in the army. He was to marry her when he got back. I wondered how that would work out. And then I was dragged out of my daydream. I had reached the spot, there was no doubt about it. The pink wallpaper told me so. But there was just a gaping hole and rubble there. There was a wooden cross in the rubble to show that there were bodies under there. What had happened? So many human stories broken off, just like that, with so much more to tell.

This did not put me in the most positive of moods for my meeting with Lexi. Indeed, I thought at first I would not find her. When I reached her street I was surrounded by a frozen sea of shattered ruins. House after house was an empty shell, not one had survived intact. But Lexi was still there, living in the ruins. She asked about Peter and I told her I was going the next day to see him. She had visited people in camps and prisons several times, including her own father. She warned me that Peter might even be shown signed confessions, fake evidence of betrayal by his friends. When I asked her about 20 July, about why Adam had not got out quickly, for I still knew so little, she told me that even in Berlin there had been little hard news. Even when news of Hitler's survival, just a few scratches, came through, people like Adam still hoped that this might trigger a revolt, something. Then it was too late. They were caught. She was sobbing when she told me the final horror. 'Chris, they hanged them slowly, one by one, from meat hooks – and they filmed them while they were dying.'

A photograph of Berlin taken in 1945. It shows the extent of the devastation caused by constant bombing. Look very carefully and you will see that some buildings that look whole at first glance are really windowless shells. People like Christabel Bielenberg's friend, Lexi, still lived in these places. They had nowhere else to go. Other cities in Germany, France and England also looked like this. Indeed, some looked worse. The German town that is said by many people to have suffered the worst devastation from bombing was not Berlin, but Dresden. Bombing had even more devastating effects in Japan. This is because Japanese houses were made of paper and wood, not brick. They were flattened by any type of bombing, because they were so flimsy.

CHAPTER 10

Ravensbrück

It was not snowing when I reached the halt for Ravensbrück, but there was an icy wind whipping across the plain. I had no idea where to go, but followed the tracks of a large official Mercedes with an SS driver and eventually a high wire fence, topped with barbed wire, loomed up beside me. There was also a wooden tower. When I looked up at it I realized the guard in the tower had a tommy gun pointing at my head. I had to pass several of these towers before I reached the barrier and was shown into a long, narrow wooden hut by the entrance. I had to wait there until my name was called. Then I was led across a square more like a military camp than a prison, round various houses and huts, then into a hut by the fence. It was some sort of office and a man in the uniform of the Security Police, called *Herr* John, came in and said this was where I would meet Peter. He was very polite. Minutes passed in silence then a tall figure passed the window. I knew it was Peter. The door opened. In came a short fat guard, then Peter himself. I jumped to my feet as he hurried towards me with hands outstretched. There was an urgent look on his face and I realized he was pressing a small hard square object into my hands. I turned my back to *Herr* John and the guard, took up my handbag and, while getting out my hankie to wipe my eyes, dropped the object into my bag. It was a matchbox. The guard motioned Peter to a bench against the wall. I quickly sat next to him and took his hand. The guard sat opposite us. *Herr* John went back to his desk at the other end of the room. We only had fifteen minutes and I had to give him my message and speak normally.

At first it seemed he was hardly listening as I babbled away about the children and this and that. I managed, by moving my hand and his, to get the message to him that there was a microphone, as well as a listening guard. And, under cover of babbling about the village and the people there, I asked him if he remembered *Frau* Muckle's sister, the one with four sons – Carl, Arnold, Adolf and another. I was squeezing his hand hard as I said this. I could not say Adam, it was too unusual a name. But he understood anyway, and when I said that Adolf was alive and Arnold, but that Carl and the other one were dead, I knew my message was understood. I had hardly remembered why I was supposed to be visiting, how Arnold had managed to get me this meeting. Then I did remember – money. So we spoke of money and Peter explained to me how to get money from Seiler in Munich for the rent, and who else to borrow from. We talked of borrowing from Arnold, all very slowly, because we both felt that if we stopped talking the interview would be ended. *Herr* John stood up and said I had to go – the interview had lasted twenty minutes. I thanked him for the extra time and asked politely for a pass out, or even a guide, as things were so confusing. He politely gave me both.

The guard said there was a 'cosy pub up the road' where I could wait for the train. It turned out to be full of SS guards; I and my matchbox went straight to the station. I was shaking when I got on the train. When I was sure no one was going to get in the compartment I shook out the few matches and tried to read the few words written on the scrap of paper in cramped writing. A string of words, which at first seemed meaningless: 'Self non-political have conceded nothing Adam close friend Hamburg days Clarita childhood Langbehn neighbour only Chris Irish Moltke lawyer together professionally wife hen food Peter Yorck – ' I could not read the last words.

When I got back Arnold and Mabel wanted to hear all about it. They seemed so glad about how it had gone, that I decided to tell them about the matchbox. At first Arnold looked amazed, then he burst out laughing. Then he became very serious. 'But why did he do it Chris? You might have been searched, it put you in great danger, which is very unlike him. Why?' I was too sleepy to think about why then. But in the middle of the night I woke and saw it clearly. He had given me this in case I was interrogated. Well, perhaps I could be. Perhaps I could arrange a meeting with Lange. I got straight up and burnt the matchbox. I knew what to do now.

A photograph of women workers, taken in Ravensbrück concentration camp. Women as well as men were put into concentration camps, and Germans as well as Jews and people from more 'degenerate' races, like Poles and Slavs. Most prisoners were given hard physical work to do in these camps. These women are digging foundations for a new building. Prisoners also worked on the farms near the camp. The picture is of poor quality. It is possible that it was taken secretly.

Chapter 11

Peter's Story

I got a message from Adam on 16 July asking when I would next be in Berlin. I knew what it meant. I had to wait until my co-director got back from Czechoslovakia – sent a message to say I could reach Berlin on 28 July – heard news on the radio on 20 July. When I got to Berlin Adam had been arrested. I tried to get news of him but no one had any. He was taken to Oranienburg. He was brought – nine thirty every morning, one of the secretaries found out – to Prinz Albrechtstrasse. Only one guard and a driver. There was only one thing to do – the factory had an **arsenal**, full of machine guns – I had a key. Get some – and a car with petrol – thought out a good place to hide him. But I hadn't been back a quarter of an hour when two Gestapo showed up – talked about security in the firm, driving me back, not sure what they knew. Then, in their office – looking down the barrels of a couple of revolvers – taken to a cell. There were just four stone walls and a bucket of water. Nothing else. Except me and the silence. I was sure my plan had been betrayed. I started to shiver – shake and shiver – I had never been frightened before – too big – now I was dead scared. I don't know how long the shivering went on – a day – a night – two days – but it stopped quite suddenly. I thought about what I was scared of – death – torture – thought about them in great detail – faced them – then the shivering stopped. It was lucky I was not interrogated in those first four days – they would have enjoyed it – I found out they did not know much – one of my clerks suspected – but no evidence.

I didn't get much to eat. A piece of bread and a mug of water morning and evening – One day they threw in another prisoner – a Pole from our factory. He was sentenced to death. We were given some beans to shell – from the garden of one of the guards – you could see it from my window – the beans were wrapped in newspaper – we read that the Allies were in France. The Pole hoped they'd be here soon enough to save him – but a day or so later he was shot. I think this was when I had been there about five or six weeks. This was all in Graudenz, then I was moved to Lehrterstrasse prison – that was where I had my first interrogations with Lange there – I hate him, if I met him I would kill him, slowly – the way he killed the others. Then we were transferred to Ravensbrück – got there some time in the evening – better cell – hot water pipe running through it and a blanket. But the cells where I was were surrounded on three sides by the women's camp. The wall under my window was a punishment wall, women were beaten there and all sorts. My cell was always full of the crying and moaning of those beaten women. There was one woman – an inmate promoted – *kapo* they were called – never without a whip in her hand. She was vile, but there were acts of great courage too. Women who came to comfort and bring water, knowing they would be punished themselves for it. We talked in passing at exercise time, out of the side of the mouth.

I knew I was going to see you – thought you'd been arrested. Passing the note was to make sure our evidence agreed. It never occurred to me that you were free and would ask to be interrogated – of course it helped – I think it probably tipped the scales. You made a big impression on Lange, I don't know if it was your get-up, or one hen-keeper to another, but he loathed me and I loathed him – but even so he advised my release. He said I'd go to a *Bewährungskompanie*, a sort of punishment squad, you run around over minefields, clearing them up – don't last long. Anyway – there it is – four days ago I was given my watch and the odd things I had had in my pocket when they arrested me. I was taken to a little office – they asked me where I was going – gave me a fistful of ration cards and a pass – I don't know why I was sent home, not to the army – I've no doubt that my regiment will be told and it won't be long before another invitation comes my way – we'll deal with that when it happens. I don't know why I'm here – people helped, you helped, bless you. Especially the ones who won't come back helped. They didn't give me away.

*A photograph taken in 1933 at Oranienburg concentration camp, near Berlin (where Adam was later taken). It shows a **roll call** being taken of political prisoners. At this early stage the camps did not have uniforms for the prisoners, nor did they shave the heads of the men and the women. Conditions were still bad, though. The work was hard and the food bad.*

CHAPTER 12

Pleading for Peter

Christabel Bielenberg shared a carriage on the train to Ravensbrück with a woman and two little girls. These were the people who were collected in the black Mercedes that she followed to the camp. During the interview with Lange, she realized that he reminded her of the girls, and thought that he must be their father.

So, when he accused her and Peter at one point of unpatriotically using a car belonging to Peter's firm to take her and her children to the railway station she was able to refer to her travelling companions and suggest that everyone does things like that sometimes. This was a useful meeting.

I had an appointment with *Kriminalrat* Lange for 11 a.m. on 4 January. He sounded surprised at my rather unorthodox offer to be interrogated, but arranged to see me in the Prinz Albrechtstrasse. Acting on Lexi's instructions I dressed very carefully for the part I was to play. She said that the Gestapo were middle-class and conventional. I should be neat and tidy, not smart, little make-up, hair in a bun. The headquarters of the Gestapo was a huge, gloomy **edifice**, partly destroyed by bombs. It was here that the green padlocked vans drew up and **disgorged** their victims. Carl, Adam, Peter and others, all climbed these stairs, hoping against hope. When I reached the third floor I was out of breath, numb with cold and shaking like a leaf. At last I reached the office door, knocked, went in. An SS man told me to wait. I was glad to sit down, to fight my rising panic by thinking of other things. Slowly this worked. The room, which had blurred, came back into focus. I was finally called into a room at the far end. This room was smaller and seemed to have arc lights behind the desk – for a moment or two I was completely blinded. '*Heil Hitler*, *Frau* Bielenberg, will you take a chair?' a high pitched voice said. '*Heil Hitler*, *Herr Kriminalrat*, I would if I could see one, but to tell the truth I can see nothing at all with these lights blazing, please turn them off.' In my panic what I had meant as a request sounded far more like a demand. There was a moment of complete silence, then the lights went off. Now I could see Lange. He was short, square, with a pear-shaped head and dark, thinning hair. His eyes were an intense, unwinking blue. I thanked him for turning off the light. He sat and stared at me across the desk. I am rather short-sighted so have never found it hard to gaze directly back at people – they are never quite in focus. I did so now. The silence lengthened. I filled it by thanking him for giving me an interview and for permission to visit Peter. I said how glad I was he was dealing with Peter's case. I had been told he was an experienced investigator, so would find the truth and free Peter.

All through the interview I had to try to sound grateful, respectful. I explained that I had asked for the interview because I feared that Peter might be in more trouble because I was seen as English. I went on to explain that I now saw myself as a German. I was on the side of the Führer, who had, after all, offered England many chances to pull out of the war. I then explained I was not English anyway, but Irish. This led to an enquiry into my English 'connections'. I took him through my English/Irish ancestry. I made it very complicated. Then I suggested that, rather than discussing my past or the problems of the Irish and the English, we should discuss Peter and his possible involvement in the Plot. Suddenly Lange's manner changed. He was no longer polite. He was shouting. He banged a big file on his desk and yelled at me that both my husband and I were fools, but he was not to be easily fooled.

'You are not a stupid woman, although you would have me believe that you are **guileless**. I have a list here of people, friends of yours, all of them traitors. You are not going to sit there and say that they were friends, visited your homes, and yet spoke nothing of politics?' This was the tricky bit. I said that we had not really talked politics at all. Neither Peter or I was interested in politics. These people were our friends, especially Adam and Clarita, who were our good friends. But we knew nothing of their politics, perhaps they found it a relief to have one house to visit where they did not have to talk politics. He pressed me on the Langbehns, my phone calls to Carl's mother, surely we were more than neighbours? I replied that we were both mothers and so I sympathized with her as such. He seemed to lose interest at this point. My mind seemed to wander in the hot stuffy room, and he talked about rationing, gardening, keeping hens. We had quite a lively discussion about the problems of feeding them. I nearly gave him the address of a hen food black marketeer!

At last he said, 'Your evidence has been interesting. It does not agree with that of your husband in any way.' I knew that to be a lie. 'Then,' I said firmly, 'I was wrong to come here, for I am a bad liar. I cannot change what I have said. If you want to know what I think it is you who should answer questions. I had thought the Führer safe in your hands, yet it took a bomb, a bomb in an air raid shelter, before you found there were enemies in the camp. A terrifying thought. Does it terrify you as it does me, *Kriminalrat*, because if it doesn't it should.' Lange sprang to his feet. 'Dear lady, the interview is at an end. I have volunteered for the army. Before I go I promise I will deal with your husband's case. I cannot tell you the outcome, but I will see it is settled before I go.' I thanked him and left. As I left the building I looked at my watch. I had been in the building for nine hours.

A photograph of the outside of the Gestapo headquarters in Prinz Albrechtstrasse. The people and guards in the foreground are in an open backed truck. They might be visiting prisoners, or arriving to be questioned. The photograph is a strange shape, and rather blurred. It is possible that it was taken with a hidden camera. The guards were very watchful, and would probably not have wanted photographs taken. During the war people did take photographs from all sorts of angles, with cameras hidden in briefcases, in handbags or in parcels. They also took pictures out of the windows of parked or slowly moving vehicles.

CHAPTER 13

Meeting on a Train

At the station, waiting for the train, I made friends with a rather fussy little man called *Herr* Lemke. We found ourselves a carriage, which we thought was empty, and began to spread ourselves about. *Herr* Lemke got out packets of sandwiches, even brandy, which all had to be black market. Then a searchlight swept the carriage. It fell on a black peaked cap, decorated with the skull and crossbones, in the opposite rack. It fell on a tall figure in a black uniform, in the corner, next to the window opposite. He was staring straight at me, still as a statue. I had time to register fair short-clipped hair, a pale, long, rather handsome face, even a curious twitch in one cheek, the only sign of life, before the searchlight swung away. *Herr* Lemke had seen him too. He offered a share of his food. It was declined in a cold, sarcastic voice. He fled the carriage.

The SS officer offered me his greatcoat to cover my knees, seeing as I was cold. I thanked him, but refused. He started to tell me that he came from Riga, a country much invaded by Poles, Swedes, Russians and Germans. He told me how he came to join the army. 'My father was killed by the Russians, and then the Germans came. We were very glad, for the Russian occupation had been hard. I looked at those soldiers and I wanted to join them, to revenge myself on the Russians. So I did.' Then he asked me where I came from. I told him that I was Irish, and he made some remark about the Irish having sympathetic voices, which is why he was telling me all this. 'They told us we could revenge ourselves on our enemies, the Poles. We went to Poland. Not to fight; they were defeated long ago. To kill Jews. We just had the shooting to do, others did the burying. Do you know what it means to kill Jews – men, women and children as they stand in a semicircle around the machine guns? I belonged to a Death Squad. I know. What do you say when I tell you that a little boy, the age of my youngest brother, stood to attention, and asked if he stood straight enough? Or the priest, the priest who stepped out of the ranks, looked at each of us in turn with a deep, dark, terrible look and said "My children, God is watching what you do." I could not forget that look.' The window I had climbed through would not close properly. It was spreading a numbing cold through the carriage. The voice, just a voice in the darkness, went on and on, sometimes so low I could hardly hear it over the noise of the train. He told me that he had resigned from the Death Squad and joined the Waffen SS, the fighting SS units. He told me how each time he fought he tried to get killed. His comrades fell around him each time while, by some miracle, he lived. The ones with the photographs in their wallets, the frightened ones, the ones with a dream of the future, they were killed. It was the ones who didn't care who got the Iron Crosses. Now he was going back to the front, to his unit or anywhere where he would be allowed to die.

During his story I found it increasingly difficult to concentrate. I had hardly eaten all day and the cold was intense. I fought wave after wave of exhaustion. 'You are silent, horrified by my story?' 'No, no,' my voice seemed far away. 'Well, I am horrified but I pity you, too, and those who have died and may have to die for you.' I was asleep. I woke twice. Once, when the train jerked to a halt at a little station, I realized that I was warmer, but that my head was resting on something hard and uncomfortable. The man had moved to sit next to me, his greatcoat over my knees. My head had fallen onto his shoulder and his SS tabs had pressed into my cheek. His hand, with the signet ring of the SS, was resting on mine and as I moved mine his had clung to it, with an almost desperate grip. I put my head back on his shoulder, gently so as not to wake him, and slept again. When I woke again the carriage was empty and the train was moving.

A photograph of Aachen, the first German town to be captured by the Allies, after its capture in 1945. It was said that Aachen was offered the choice to surrender or die. They in fact had no choice. The Nazis were offering them the choice of fighting or dying. This picture shows the American 1st Division with German soldiers who surrendered after the Americans entered the city.

CHAPTER 14

Waiting for the End

One morning Sepp's voice brought me to the window, '*Frau Dr, Frau Dr*, good news!' I went to meet him. His face was glowing with delight. '*Herr Dr* rang up in the night, all the way from Berlin, he is free.' I found myself hugging him, crying with delight, and he was hugging me, and we were laughing and crying and stood there so long that my sock froze to the ground. The next two days passed in a whirl of organized pandemonium. I had to tidy up, turn over a new leaf. In the course of this I did find time to wonder how on earth a knife and fork and a perfectly good bicycle pump found their way into the spinet. John took advantage of the tidying up and my air of elation to persuade me to let him take my gramophone to pieces, to make a machine for winding wool with. I would willingly have allowed him to transform it into a moon rocket, had he asked. The radio brought us news through the day that there were fresh batches of Allied planes over Germany. I concentrated on a train heading from Berlin to Rohrbach – please God making steady, uninterrupted progress.

A poster for using the radio. The slogan reads: 'All of Germany listens to the Führer on national radio.' Maybe they did, but the radio had another significance as well. It was possible to tune in to foreign radio stations, to hear the news and other things, even just dance music, rather than the stream of propaganda that flooded out of the national radio. Of course the other countries knew this was happening. The British also used the radio as propaganda. It would not necessarily be the truth that people heard as they sat listening to the banned foreign radio stations, with an ear pressed right up against the set so that they did not have to have it on too loud. Especially in the last days of the war, the radio was the quickest – sometimes the only – way of finding out what was happening.

Ganz Deutschland hört den Führer

mit dem Volksempfänger

But by the afternoon of the following day Peter had still not come. I began to get jittery. There was something on the radio about able bodied men not being allowed to leave Berlin, a last minute stand. Surely not Peter? But the evening train should have arrived by now. The children, washed and dressed up in clean pyjamas for the occasion, would have to go to bed. Just as I was tucking Nicky in I heard a faint sound. I rushed to the window, straining my ears. I had not been mistaken. It was Peter, yodelling from down the valley. I closed the window and turned to Nicky. 'I think I heard a yodel from down in the valley,' I said. 'I think it may be Daddy.'

It was indeed Peter. He arrived and the children all tumbled out of bed and all over him. Then they were dispatched to bed again and *Frau* Muckle appeared with a huge frying pan, full of eggs and bacon, at least ten eggs. It was not exactly what a doctor would have prescribed for a man who had lived so long on bread and water, but Peter polished off nine of the eggs and most of the bacon, and a great deal of coffee. Then he told me what had happened. He told me everything, in detail. I knew I would probably never hear it again. As he talked he paced the floor, four paces by four paces, the dimension of his prison cell. All through the night he talked and talked, until he talked himself to a standstill. When he had finished he stopped pacing and went to lean out of the window, looking over the valley. 'I'm here Chris, and here I stay, nothing can make me leave again.'

Yet, despite this, things conspired to try to get him to leave. He was sick and weak from his imprisonment. He was hardly well again when his regiment demanded that he report for duty at Mariendorf, east of Berlin. Peter left the letter a few days, then replied that he had no money, could they let him have a travel permit. This gave him a few more days grace, but then he received orders to get a pass from the Army railway station patrol. Peter replied that our station did not have such a patrol. By then we had reached the middle of March. The news coming through on the radio suggested that the Allies were still gaining, they had crossed the Rhine at Remagen, yet they were moving so slowly. We were still in the Third Reich, Peter still had to obey orders. We could not go on stalling forever. **Deserters** and stragglers, the radio dispassionately announced, were being rounded up and shot, with those who could give no valid reason for not being with their units. Peter got a telegram telling him to report at once.

The war was bearing down on Rohrbach too, the soldiers' war. The local paper gave up the ghost, no more ink, no more paper. Now there was just the radio. The villagers still went about their farming business, despite the fighter bombers, the trenches dug in the fields, the Army Medical Unit billeted in the village itself.

LAST WEEKS OF THE WAR

The last weeks of the war were remarkable mainly for Hitler's refusal to accept defeat. Even when the Russians were just outside Berlin, Hitler was calling on old men and boys as young as fourteen to fight. He had not been seen, in person, since April. But, in the end, even he saw defeat was inevitable.

Many people think Hitler committed suicide in his safety bunker in Berlin, the day before the Russians captured the city. Certainly a body was found, a burned body that had signs of having taken poison. There was a lot of talk that Hitler had faked his death and escaped to South America. South America certainly became a hiding place for a good many Nazis. Others were arrested and tried for 'war crimes' in a series of trials held in the German town of Nuremberg.

WHATEVER HAPPENED TO...?

Frau Muckle stayed in Rohrbach after the war. So did Martina, Hans the milkman, the mayor and Sepp Kern.

Arnold survived the war. He and Mabel moved to Munich, where he started up his own business.

Lexi was arrested in March 1945, but survived until the Allies arrived in Berlin. She married, moved to Spain and died in 1968.

Christabel and Peter Bielenberg moved with their children to Ireland. They still live there. Christabel became a British citizen again.

Peter knew he had only one card to play. He had to be too sick to travel. He needed a warrant from an army doctor. We chose a doctor, fat and comfortable looking, who had confided to Hans over a game of cards that he had civilian clothes in his luggage and had no intention of being captured by the French. Peter and I tried to think what illness he could have. The village doctor said he'd give Peter a malaria injection that would send his temperature soaring. The army doctor was to be fetched when it rose. Peter's temperature did indeed rise, as high as 106°F. I went to fetch the army doctor. He was unimpressed, saying he would come later. Later? That might be too late. I went back to Peter. He was still very sick-looking. An hour later his temperature was going down. I went and sobbed over the doctor, and, unwillingly, he came and examined Peter thoroughly. His fever was falling fast. 'What do you want of me?' he asked. Peter, never a good liar, told him. 'I was released from a concentration camp some weeks back, and have been ordered back to my unit. I want you to sign a sickness warrant for me.' There was a moment of complete silence. Then the doctor agreed.

The warrant gave Peter a few days, but we knew he would have to go into hiding. He had been moving things into the woods from the day that the first telegram arrived. The mayor, Sepp and the two older boys were the only people, other than *Frau* Muckle, Hans and Martina, who knew of the plan. The children took food up to him. I stayed below, cooking tasteless food with smaller and smaller rations. Ordinary life was grinding to a standstill. No soap, paper, pencils, thread, nothing. No privacy either. Our rooms were full of soldiers, sleeping in heaps everywhere, weary boys in outsized uniforms, armed with weapons they did not even have the sense to handle with care. Chased from pillar to post, only able to travel at night, unable to understand why they were not allowed to give in, they were a very different army from the one that that fanned outwards over Europe so confidently five years back. A grey-faced, red-eyed sergeant looking down at his sleeping charges said, 'Those swine at the top have committed many crimes, but none greater than sending the babies in to fight.'

Everyone now was grumpy, tired, uncooperative, even selfish. Everyone was closing in around their own needs and concerns. It seemed as though it would go on forever. Then, after a few quite days, the storm broke. There was fierce shelling in the night. On opening the window in the morning I found the village had become an armed camp. Every farmhouse had an army vehicle lodged at its side, covered by logs of fir branches. The heavy artillery was being hauled by horses or oxen towards the forest, followed by gunners and carts of ammunition. Staff cars drew up outside the *Adler*, the generals moved in. As soon as I could I sent Nicky to tell Peter what was going on. That night Peter slipped down to Hans' house.

We went to see him the next morning, only to see the mayor coming up the hill with two military police. We were sure they had found out about Peter. They had come, it turned out, to commandeer his bike. Two more days limped by. The generals had the radio, we heard no news. Our village became the scene of shootings; of deserters, even civilians who refused to help. Then, finally, the soldiers pulled out of the village, blowing up all they could not use as they went.

It took all of forty-eight hours for the village to decide that German, French or American, the early potatoes still needed to go in. At night, straggling remnants of German troops still trickled through the valley. Then we heard on the radio that Hitler had killed himself. One day I met a woman in the street who had obviously been scavenging. She looked Russian. I asked her, she nodded. 'Du?' she asked. A good question, really. 'Oh, Ingelski, or something,' I said and we shook hands. Somehow I was both laughing and crying and so I celebrated our **liberation**, on 2 May, 1945.

Russian soldiers erecting their flag on the top of the Reichstag building, on 2 May, 1945. In the background, behind the soldier reaching for the flag, you can see the Russian tanks on the streets of Berlin.

Glossary

All definitions refer to Christabel Bielenberg's use of the word in the 1930s and 40s.

Allies allies are people from different countries who agree to fight together. When used with a capital 'A' it means the alliance of Britain and other countries to fight Germany in the Second World War. The membership of the Allies changed during the war. Britain was always a member. France was, until captured by Germany. Russia joined later in the war, as did America.

allotment a small part of a large piece of land which is rented out to grow things on.

aquavit an alcoholic drink, yellow or colourless, made from potatoes.

arsenal a weapon store.

Aryan a word taken from an old word for 'noble'. In Nazi Germany it was applied to people who had no ancestors who were Jewish or came from an 'inferior' race.

civilian a person who is not in the armed forces.

cobbler a person who mends shoes and boots.

concentration camp a sort of prison camp, for civilians, not soldiers. They were first set up by the British in South Africa, in the 1880s, but then used more extensively in Nazi Germany. (See box on page 34 and pictures on pages 35 and 37.)

cordoned off separated up by ropes or barriers of some kind.

coupons ration books had coupons, slips of paper that you needed to be allowed to buy food.

crayfish a small lobster.

decadent something that is rotten, past its best.

decreed passed a law.

depression this refers to the economic depression which swept the western world at the time. People lost money, factories went out of business, people lost their jobs and prices went up.

deserters people who run away from the army.

detention camps prisons for civilians. Mostly used to keep political opponents all in one place.

dialect a slightly different version of a language, spoken in a particular part of the country. So people in Yorkshire and Devon, for example, speak English in a different way from people in London.

dilapidated falling down.

disconnect telephones were, at this time, connected to the telephone point by a removable cord. This could be taken out to 'disconnect' it.

disgorge literally means 'throw out', unload is the sense here.

edifice something that has been built.

Embassy a place in one country where representatives from another country live. It is treated as a part of the country that owns the Embassy. Embassies can only be set up if both countries agree to it.

evacuees people who have moved out of their homes, temporarily, to live somewhere else. Often they go because they are ordered to by the government.

Fatherland Germany.

fidelity fatihfulness.

guileless unable to lie or pretend.

Himmler Himmler was the head of the SS (see box on page 10). On Hitler's orders, he set up the Death Camps for disposing of the Jews (see box on page 40).

incline a gradual upward slope.

inconsistency not behaving or thinking in the same way all the time.

inflation where money loses its value and become worth less and less. In a period of inflation prices rise rapidly.

iniquitous wicked, unjust and outrageous.

kirsch an alcoholic drink, made from cherry stones.

liberation being set free.

mass a Catholic Church service.

master race Hitler and the Nazis used this to describe 'pure' Germans (see **Aryans**).

mutual something that groups of people share. Mutual friends, in this case, are people who were friends of both the Bielenbergs and the Langbehns before they became friends with each other.

negotiations talks between two or more people or groups who do not necessarily want the same thing, to reach an agreement that satisfies everyone.

number each person serving in the army, navy or air force of a country is given a number. People serving in armed forces are often told that if they are captured they should only tell the enemy their name and number.

ousted removed from a position of power.

paraphernalia all the things that are needed for a uniform, or a performance or a religious service etc.

patrolling walking around an area, looking out for suspicious people or things.

propaganda spreading ideas or beliefs that a particular group want to be believed. Propaganda is used a lot by rival countries in war-time, to trick the other side into thinking they are losing, or that attacks will happen in one place not another. It can also be used in peace-time, as Hitler and the Nazis used it, to get people to believe Nazi ideas. Propaganda can be spread in many ways, including radio, pictures, speeches, newspapers articles and books, even in schools as lessons. (See boxes on pages 17 and 25.)

punchline the bit at the end of a long story that goes, 'And the funny thing was...'.

rationing limiting the amount of something that people can use or buy. In war time food, petrol and other vital things were rationed by governments. In some places, for example cities that were cut off from food supplies by the enemy, food and water was rationed by the people in charge of the city.

Red Cross the Red Cross is an organization that works in all countries to help the wounded and bring food supplies to refugees or prisoners of war. The Geneva Convention, a treaty about how war should be conducted that most countries keep to, states that Red Cross vehicles cannot be attacked.

refugees people fleeing from one place to another, because of war, or because of their political or religious beliefs. Unlike evacuees, who are usually ordered to move away and expect to return to their homes, refugees mostly choose to go and do not expect to return.

Reichstag the name for the German Parliament and also the name of the building in Berlin where the Parliament met.

resplendent magnificent, dazzlingly bright.

roll call the daily, or even more frequent, reading out of the names of prisoners. Prisoners have to answer to their name, to check that everyone is still in the prison.

shrapnel parts of a bomb that has burst. The bomb explodes and the pieces of the bomb go in all directions.

sirens horns or hooters that make a distinctive noise when there is likely to be a bombing raid. When people hear the siren they go to somewhere where it is safe.

smarted felt cross about.

sold down the river tricked.

spinet a type of piano.

Star of David a six-pointed star, drawn as two triangles, one upright, one upside down. It was used as a symbol to show that people were Jewish.

stirrup pump a small pump, worked by pushing up and down with a foot. It was used to put out small fires.

storm-troopers Hitler's unofficial army, his brown-shirted supporters.

swastika the symbol of the Nazi party, a cross with each of the arms of the cross bent forwards at 45 degrees.

thrifty careful about not being wasteful.

virtuous behaving well.

wanton irresponsible, thoughtless, destructive.

Index

Numbers in *italic* type refer to pictures and captions; numbers in **bold** type refer to information boxes.